30 Questions Librarians Ask about Taping Copyrighted Television Programs for Educational Use

Interpreting the Guidelines for Off-Air Recording

30 Questions Librarians Ask about Taping Copyrighted Television Programs for Educational Use

Interpreting the Guidelines for Off-Air Recording

Washington Office
American Library Association

American Library Association / Chicago

Designed by Ellen Pettengell

Text composed in IBM Selectric Prestige Elite
by Vladimir Reichl & Associates.
Display type composed in American Typewriter
Medium Condensed by Total Typography, Inc.

Printed on 50-pound Antique Glatfelter,
a pH-neutral stock, and bound in 65-pound
Hammermill cover stock by Imperial Printing Co.

Library of Congress Cataloging in Publication Data
Main entry under title:

30 questions librarians ask about taping copyrighted
television programs for educational use.

1. Fair use (Copyright)--United States--Miscellanea.
2. Copyright--Broadcasting rights--United States--
Miscellanea. I. American Library Association. Washington Office. II. Title: Thirty questions librarians
ask about taping ...

KF3030.95.A13	346.7304'82	82-8691
ISBN 0-8389-3274-6	347.306482	AACR2

Printed in the United States of America.

Third printing, March 1984

Contents

Introduction

The last several years have seen dramatic new developments in the technology of copying material transmitted via broadcast media. These developments have presented Congress with massive problems in reconciling the conflicting claims of copyright owners, TV networks, performance guilds, and potential users of copyrighted broadcasts, especially librarians, teachers and scholars.

Ever since Public Law 94-553, *General Revision of the Copyright Law*, was enacted in 1976, there has been a wide divergence of views on the proper application of the new law to the off-air recording of television broadcasts. In that act, Congress for the first time specifically recognized in the legislative history of the new law that off-air taping of commercial and noncommercial television broadcasts for nonprofit educational use by teachers in classrooms *may* be fair use. The problem comes in determining the scope of fair use in this context. What does fair use of off-air recordings mean?

Because the new copyright law was not clear as to what constituted fair use and because Congressional committees did not incorporate a resolution of the divergent views into the act, Representative Robert C. Kastenmeier, chair of the House Subcommittee on Courts, Civil Liberties and the Administration of Justice, appointed in March 1979 a negotiating committee of nineteen educational users and copyright proprietors to write guidelines applying the fair use provision of the copyright law to the recording, retention, and use of television programs for educational purposes.

The negotiating committee met intermittently over a two-year period to resolve their differences and on September 28, 1981, the agreed-upon guidelines were presented to the House Subcommittee. These "safe harbor" guidelines for off-air taping of copyrighted programs were officially recognized on October 14 when they were inserted in the *Congressional Rec-*

ord by Representative Kastenmeier. In presenting the guidelines to Congress, the Subcommittee chair stated that he "shared the view of the negotiating committee that these guidelines reach an appropriate balance between the proprietary rights of copyright owners and the instructional needs of educational institutions."

Rep. Kastenmeier noted that the guidelines, in his judgment, would "go a long way toward resolving the lingering problems associated with off-air videotaping of copyright works for educational purposes." He also noted that three previous sets of guidelines had already been agreed upon and were published as part of the official legislative history of the act. These guidelines covered (1) classroom copying of books and periodicals in nonprofit educational institutions, (2) educational uses of music, and (3) photocopying by libraries. The newest guidelines (on off-air taping of copyrighted broadcast programs) would become the fourth set of guidelines to define fair use in certain situations. In House Report 94-1476, p. 72, the House Judiciary Committee stated that the three previous guidelines "are a reasonable interpretation of the minimum standards of fair use. Teachers will know that copying within the guidelines is fair use. Thus, the guidelines serve the purpose of filling the need for greater certainty and protection for teachers."

As in the case of the three previous guidelines, the off-air taping guidelines are considered to be "a reasonable interpretation" of the meaning of fair use when applied to the taping off-air of television broadcast programs for educational use.

Too often in the past, librarians and teachers have been reluctant or hesitant to exercise their rights of fair use under the law for fear of courting an infringement suit. It is important to understand that in United States law, copyright is a limited statutory monopoly which involves the privilege to restrict as well as to monopolize the diffusion of knowledge; hence, the public's *right* to use materials must be protected. Safeguards, such as these guidelines, have been written into the legislative history accompanying the new copyright law to protect librarians, teachers, researchers, and scholars as they carry out their responsibilities for educating all the people or for conducting research. These safeguards not only better enable them to carry out the responsibilities for which they are employed but guarantee their rights, as citizens of the United States, of access to information for teaching and learning purposes. It is, therefore, important to heed the advice of a former U.S. Register of Copyrights: "If you don't *use* fair use, you will *lose* it!"

30 Questions Librarians Ask

The questions which follow are designed to answer some of the inquiries which librarians are making regarding the educational guidelines for off-air taping.

Fair Use and the Guidelines (General)

1. *What is meant by "fair use" of copyrighted materials?*

   Fair use has been defined as the right to use copyrighted materials in a reasonable manner without consent of the author or copyright owner and without licensing or payment of royalties. Fair use has been called one of the most important limitations on the copyright owner's exclusive rights and has been described as the court-developed doctrine that permits teachers, librarians, researchers, scholars, and others to use copyrighted works without paying the copyright holder. Fair use was written into the law for the first time in 1976. Section 107 of the new copyright law (PL 94-553), which went into effect January 1, 1978, spells out four criteria which must be considered in determining whether the use made of a work in any particular case is a fair use:

   (1) the purpose and character of the use, including whether such use is of a commercial nature or is for nonprofit educational purposes;
   (2) the nature of the copyrighted work;
   (3) the amount and substantiality of the portion used in relation to the copyrighted work as a whole; and
   (4) the effect of the use upon the potential market for or value of the copyrighted work.

2. *Does the doctrine of "fair use" apply to nonprint materials as well as print?*

   Yes. Fair use applies to all types of materials, print and nonprint. The House Judiciary Committee (in House Report 94-1476) commented as follows:

   > The problem of off-the-air taping for non-profit classroom use of copyrighted audiovisual works incorporated in radio and television broadcasts has proved to be difficult to resolve. The Committee believes that the fair use doctrine has some limited application in this area, but it appears that the development of detailed guidelines will require a more thorough exploration than has so far been possible of the needs and problems of a number of different interests affected, and of the various legal problems presented.

   The "detailed guidelines" which the committee refers to above are those which are presented herewith in Appendix A.

3. *Do the guidelines have the force of law?*

   No, they do not have the same force as law but they can be very influential in court cases. The courts give great deference to private agreements jointly arrived at by both parties in a dispute and to current business practices.

4. *The educational guidelines seem to be directed largely to teachers and the classroom situation. How do they affect librarians?*

   If you are a librarian serving students and instructors in classrooms, these guidelines affect you directly. If you are a librarian in a library open to the public, these guidelines--combined with section 107 references to scholarship and research--set forth reasonable standards for application in your library. Furthermore, libraries and archives already have permission in the 1976 law to copy news programs off the air, as indicated in section 108(f)(3) and (h). The concept of "teacher" in the guidelines on print materials was intended by Congress to be defined broadly to include "instructional specialists working in consultation with actual instructors." The term "instructional specialists" would, of course, include instructional media specialists and librarians who are library-media coordinators.

5. *Do the guidelines apply to higher education institutions as well as to elementary-secondary schools?*

   Yes, even though the focus seems to be on elementary-secondary schools. Both the American Council on Education, the American Association of University Professors, and the National Education Association support the guidelines.

6. *Do the guidelines apply to all educational users even if their organization did not have a representative on the committee that developed the guidelines?*

   In our judgment, the House Committee did not say that these were reasonable guidelines for the signatories only. They are meant to apply to all educational users insofar as the House Committee endorsed the guidelines and introduced them into the *Congressional Record* as the product of "a negotiating committee of interested parties, *developed by the Judiciary Committee*," and urged "their widest possible dissemination" (emphasis added). As such, there is a clear intent of the chairman of the House Committee that this agreement be placed in the same context as the three other educational agreements negotiated so far.

7. *Do these guidelines invalidate contractual arrangements which schools or libraries make with copyright owners when they obtain copies or recordings of works for their school or library collections?*

   No, any contractual obligations assumed when the library or archives obtained the copy or phonorecord of a work in its collection must be honored. In view of this, librarians must be especially sensitive to the conditions under which they purchase materials. Before executing an agreement which would limit their rights under the copyright law, librarians should seek legal counsel through their administrators. Contractual obligations are made over and above the copyright law; hence, they must be honored first by the contracting parties. Therefore, as section 108(f)(4) of the 1976 revision of the Copyright Act clearly indicates, watch what you sign!

Scope of the Guidelines

8. *What materials do these guidelines cover?*

   They cover copyrighted television programs *broadcast*

on commercial and noncommercial stations for reception by the general public without charge.

9. *Is everything on television copyrighted?*

   Works created before January 1, 1978, which have been copyrighted will contain a copyright symbol (a letter "c" in a circle, the word "Copyright," or the abbreviation "Copr.") with the year. If the work was produced before January 1, 1978, it is unprotected unless it bears a copyright symbol. Copyright notice requirements have been relaxed since 1978, so that the absence of notice on a work created after January 1, 1978 does not necessarily mean the work is in the public domain.

10. *Under the guidelines, can you tape cable television programs?*

    Yes, if the program is a retransmission or if cable is the only redistribution method available in your community.

    No, if the program is on pay television (e.g., Home Box Office).

11. *Do the guidelines apply to the off-air taping of radio programs?*

    No. They cover only television programs broadcast over the air. The negotiating committee limited its discussions to television only.

12. *Do the guidelines set forth strict limits on copying by teachers or librarians?*

    As pointed out in the "Advisory Statement of the Ad Hoc Committee on Copyright Law" (Educational Users) in Appendix B of this pamphlet, the committee recognizes that "there are likely to be instances in which adherence to the letter of these guidelines would interfere with legitimate needs of educational procedures. In pursuit of those needs, particular educators may deem uses beyond the guidelines to be necessary, fair, and within the law. They must recognize also, however, that the copyright owners, for their part, are not constrained by these guidelines to refrain from a claim of infringement in such instances."

Off-Air Copying--Specific Interpretations

13. *Can the librarian copy a program off the air for a teacher?*

    Yes, provided the teacher requested the librarian to do so. The librarian may not copy the program in anticipation that a teacher may request the program. After the date of recording, the program must be used during the first 10 consecutive school days in the 45-calendar-day retention period.

14. *Can the librarian tape a program off the air for an individual researcher?*

    The guidelines do not deal with this specifically, but the ALA believes that this is permissible. Section 107 of the 1976 law provides that "the fair use of a copyrighted work . . ." for purposes such as criticism, comment, news reporting, teaching, scholarship, or *research* is not an infringement of copyright (emphasis added).

15. *How long can a library keep a program copied off the air?*

    The library may keep the program 45 consecutive calendar days after date of recording. After this time period, the program must be erased.

16. *In Guideline #3, what is the meaning of the phrase, "Off-air recordings may be used once by individual teachers in the course of relevant teaching activities"?*

    This means that a teacher may use the recording one time in each of his or her classes during the first 10 consecutive school days after date of recording. The recorded program may be used a second time in any given class to clarify points which may not have been clear or where a second showing is needed to reinforce an instructional objective. A second showing is often needed to justify purchase of that program by the school district or university for its own permanent collections.

17. *What is the purpose of the 45-day retention period?*

    The purpose is two-fold: (1) to enable teachers and librarians to use the program once in each of their classes and repeat once only when instructional reinforcement is necessary; (2) to enable teachers and librarians to explore every avenue possible to test the program material with classes before purchase, license, or rental of the program to ensure that the program adequately achieves the objectives of the instructor, student, or researcher.

18. *How is it possible for several teachers of the same subject to use a given program in their classes during the first 10 consecutive days in the retention period?*

    Guideline #5 permits the teacher/librarian or instructional media specialist to make a limited number of copies from each off-air recording to meet the legitimate instructional needs of teachers in a given building during the first 10 consecutive school days in the 45 calendar days after date of recording. Each of these copies must, however, be erased after the 45-day retention period.

19. *Does a library which is open to the public have the right to tape news programs off the air?*

    Yes, the 1976 Copyright Act specifically authorizes libraries or archives to copy news programs off the air (PL 94-553, Sec. 108[f][3]).

20. *Can an off-air recording be added to your library collection?*

    No, unless it is a copy of a news program.

21. *It is often impossible to show an entire television program recorded off-the-air within a 45-minute class period. Can excerpts of this program be shown to the class or must the program be viewed in its entirety or not used at all?*

    Guideline #7 is explicit on this point. Excerpts can be used provided the recorded program is not altered from its original content. The integrity of the program must be maintained.

22. *Can copyright holders or others who own or have purchased the rights for given television programs deny access under these guidelines for educational users of any television program?*

    The publication of the guidelines by the Congress demonstrates that it is the intent of Congress that the educational users provided for by the guidelines are intended as an exception to the otherwise exclusive rights of the copyright owner. Under the fair use provisions of the law, the copyright owner has no right to deny educational users access to any program used in keeping with the conditions spelled out in these guidelines. Rights are given under law, not by individuals.

23. *Must the proprietor make available rights to the material after fair use? That is, does the proprietor have to make the program available for rental or sale after the fair use period?*

No. The proprietor (copyright owner) has the exclusive right under the Copyright Act to do what he or she wishes with the program after or beyond fair use.

Home Recording

24. *Can individuals in the privacy of their homes tape radio programs off the air?*

The new copyright law makes no mention of home taping of sound recordings. The House Committee Report on the *Sound Recording Amendment of 1971* does apply, however. It contains a pronouncement which is relevant to this situation:

> In approving the creation of a limited copyright in sound recordings it is the intention of the Committee that this limited copyright not grant any broader rights than are accorded to other copyright proprietors under the existing title 17. Specifically, it is not the intention of the Committee to restrain the home recording, from broadcasts or from tapes or records, of recorded performances, where the home recording is for private use and with no purpose of reproducing or otherwise capitalizing commercially on it. This practice is common and unrestrained today, and the record producers and performers would be in no different position from that of the owners of copyright in recorded musical compositions over the past 20 years. (H.Rept. 92-487, p. 7)

Inasmuch as this *Sound Recording Amendment* has *not* been superseded by any other piece of legislation, it is still in effect and is the law of the land.

25. *Do these guidelines apply to video recordings made at home?*

Making video recordings at home has been a widely accepted practice which has only recently been ruled as a potential infringement of the copyright law by the 9th U.S. Circuit Court of Appeals. This matter is still in litigation in the courts. However, because the *Sound Recording Amendment of 1971* is still in effect, as pointed out in #24, for sound recordings, it is logical to assume that the same rule would apply to video recordings. It is difficult to understand why Congress would legislate one way for sound recordings and another way for video.

26. *Is it permissible for a teacher or librarian to tape a television program off the air at home and bring it to school the next day to play it back to the class?*

Yes. In fact, this may be the only way a program aired during the evening or at out-of-school hours can be taped simultaneously with the broadcast transmission or simultaneous cable retransmission, as required by the guidelines.

Infringement

27. *In case of an alleged infringement, what protection do educators and librarians have?*

If there is a school district, library, or university policy or regulation regarding taping, and the librarian or instructor is conforming to that policy or regulation, then the librarian or teacher should be protected by the library, school district, or university. Whether or not there is such a policy, the new law includes, for the first time, an "innocent infringer" provision under section 504(c)(2) which reads in part:

> The court shall remit statutory damages in any case where an infringer believed and had reasonable grounds for believing that his or her use of the copyrighted work was a fair use under section 107, if the infringer was: (i) an employee or agent of a nonprofit educational institution, library, or archives acting within the scope of his or her employment who, or such institution, li-

brary, or archives itself, which infringed by reproducing the work in copies or phonorecords;

. . .

In explaining this provision, the House Judiciary Committee intended that "the burden of proof with respect to the defendant's good faith should rest on the plaintiff." (H.Rept. 94-1476)

28. *What are the penalties if the court finds the teacher or librarian knowingly infringed the copyright?*

Under the new law, and except for the innocent-infringer provision described in section 504(c)(2), copyright infringement can result in an injunction against further violations, impoundment of wrongfully duplicated materials, actual damages suffered or "statutory" civil damages of not less than $250 and no more than $10,000 per violation, and assessment of attorneys' fees. If the violation is extraordinary, the statutory damages can be increased to $50,000. For willful violations undertaken for financial gain, criminal penalties also can be levied. First offenders may be imprisoned for up to one year and fined up to $25,000, in addition to all the civil penalties just enumerated.

29. *In case of an alleged infringement who would be sued--the librarian, the teacher who requested the copy, the school principal, the superintendent, or the school board or library board?*

Clearly, the librarian and/or the teacher can be sued, but the school district or university may also be sued. The person who does the infringing is the prime offender.

30. *Can someone not a party to this agreement file suit against a librarian or teacher for conducting activities clearly within the guidelines?*

Yes, because no one can be stopped from filing a suit, no matter how frivolous! Even though anyone can file a suit, the guidelines still apply and will be very influential in any court case. The chances of the plaintiff recovering damages would be very slim. Further, the educational community has promised to come to the support of educational users in the event of such suit.

Appendix A

Guidelines for Off-Air Recording of Broadcast Programming for Educational Use

In March 1979, Congressman Robert Kastenmeier, Chairman of the House Subcommittee on Courts, Civil Liberties and Administration of Justice, appointed a Negotiating Committee consisting of representatives of education organizations, copyright proprietors, and creative guilds and unions. The following guidelines reflect the Negotiating Committee's consensus as to the application of "fair use" to the recording, retention, and use of television broadcast programs for educational purposes. They specify periods of retention and use of such off-air recordings in classrooms and similar places devoted to instruction and for home-bound instruction. The purpose of establishing these guidelines is to provide standards for both owners and users of copyrighted television programs.

1. The guidelines were developed to apply only to off-air recording by nonprofit educational institutions.

2. A broadcast program may be recorded off-air simultaneously with broadcast transmission (including simultaneous cable retransmission) and retained by a nonprofit educational institution for a period not to exceed the first forty-five (45) consecutive calendar days after date of recording. Upon conclusion of such retention period, all off-air recordings must be erased or destroyed immediately. "Broadcast programs" are television programs transmitted by television stations for reception by the general public without charge.

3. Off-air recordings may be used once by individual teachers in the course of relevant teaching activities, and repeated once only when instructional reinforcement is necessary, in classrooms and similar places devoted to instruction within a single build-

ing, cluster or campus, as well as in the homes of students receiving formalized home instruction, during the first ten (10) consecutive school days in the forty-five (45) day calendar day retention period. "School days" are school session days--not counting weekends, holidays, vacations, examination periods, or other scheduled interruptions--within the forty-five (45) calendar day retention period.

4. Off-air recordings may be made only at the request of and used by individual teachers and may not be regularly recorded in anticipation of requests. No broadcast program may be recorded off-air more than once at the request of the same teacher, regardless of the number of times the program may be broadcast.

5. A limited number of copies may be reproduced from each off-air recording to meet the legitimate needs of teachers under these guidelines. Each such additional copy shall be subject to all provisions governing the original recording.

6. After the first ten (10) consecutive school days, off-air recordings may be used up to the end of the forty-five (45) calendar day retention period only for teacher evaluation purposes, *i.e.*, to determine whether or not to include the broadcast program in the teaching curriculum, and may not be used in the recording institution for student exhibition or any other nonevaluation purpose without authorization.

7. Off-air recordings need not be used in their entirety, but the recorded programs may not be altered from their original content. Off-air recordings may not be physically or electronically combined or merged to constitute teaching anthologies or compilations.

8. All copies of off-air recordings must include the copyright notice on the broadcast program as recorded.

9. Educational institutions are expected to establish appropriate control procedures to maintain the integrity of these guidelines.

Appendix B

Statement of Ad Hoc Committee on Off-Air Recording Guidelines

Ad Hoc Committee on Copyright Law

A Coalition of Nonprofit Organizations Representing Education, Libraries, and Scholars

The Ad Hoc Committee on Copyright Law is pleased to announce that an agreement has been reached on guidelines for off-air recordings of television programs for educational use.

Wide divergence of views on the proper application of the copyright law to off-the-air recordings of television broadcasts characterized the period of development of the Copyright Act of 1976. Congressman Robert C. Kastenmeier of the House Subcommittee on Courts, Civil Liberties and Administration of Justice appointed a negotiating group consisting of representatives of some twenty-five organizations with off-air taping interests. The organizations are diverse in nature, ranging from producers of copyright materials, creative guilds, and owners of copyright materials to those representing all of education.

The guidelines reflect the consensus of the committee members on an effective and acceptable application of "fair use" to off-air recording and use in schools of broadcast television programs for educational purposes. It must be noted, however, that not all of the representatives of copyright proprietors agreed to the new guidelines, and that some educational representatives expressed reservations about their scope.

In accepting this agreement, copyright owner representatives have agreed that copying and use of broadcasts that conform with the agreed guidelines should not be the subject of claims of infringement by copyright owners. The representatives of the education community have agreed that the educational community must live up to the spirit of the law, and that we must be responsible in a major way for monitoring educational practices.

The committee negotiators of this agreement cannot, of course, change the Copyright Law as enacted by Congress or bind any court to a particular interpretation of that law. Their joint issuance of these guidelines, however, reflects their carefully considered view of how the law can be satisfactorily applied in the mutual interest of the proprietors, the disseminators, the teachers, and the students. From the point of view of educators generally, it is recognized that there are likely to be instances in which adherence to the letter of these guidelines would interfere with legitimate needs of educational procedures. In pursuit of those needs, particular educators may deem uses beyond the guidelines to be appropriate, fair, and within the law. It must also be recognized, however, that individual copyright owners, for their part, are not constrained by these guidelines to refrain from a claim of infringement in what they consider to be unfair application of the agreed upon guidelines.

It must be emphasized that even though these guidelines are not law, the courts will look with great deference to them in any infringement action. Courts will always look to the state of the art and common business practice when interpreting an unclear legal matter. Therefore, the guidelines are especially important.

The Ad Hoc Committee alerts its membership that the guidelines contained in the agreement *only* apply to copyright materials. Programs that are not copyrighted do not enjoy the protection of the guidelines. They may be copied in toto and kept literally forever.

Similarly, the Ad Hoc Committee urges all of its members to be on the alert and to report any instances where a copyright proprietor tries to restrict the application of these guidelines.

8389-3274-6